D1297695

phi alpha gamma

BOOKS BY DAN BERNITT
AVAILABLE FROM SAWYER HOUSE

Dose: Plays & Monologues

INCLUDES:
Almost
Thanks for the Scabies, Jerkface!
Button-Down Showgirl
My Parents Talk to Stuffed Animals

Phi Alpha Gamma

phi alpha gamma

dan bernitt

SAWYER HOUSE
LEXINGTON
2008

SAWYER HOUSE
PO BOX 1415, LEXINGTON, KY 40588-1415

FIRST EDITION, December 2008

Publisher's Cataloging-in-Publication Data
Bernitt, Dan (1986–).
    Phi alpha gamma / by Dan Bernitt. —1st ed.
      p. cm.
    ISBN-13: 978-0-9821560-0-1
    ISBN-10: 0-9821560-0-6
    I. Title.

Library of Congress Control Number: 2008908935

Cover photograph © 2008 by Deogracias Lerma;
Cover photo edited by Ray Bruwelheide.
Author photograph © 2006 by Vidyuta Rangnekar.

www.sawyerhouse.net

for my father

PHI ALPHA GAMMA

"... understanding the Greek system is part of understanding America."

ALAN D. DESANTIS, *Inside Greek U.*

❧

"Do not believe that he who seeks to comfort you lives untroubled among the simple and quiet words that sometimes do you good. His life has much difficulty and sadness. ... Were it otherwise he would never have been able to find those words."

RAINER MARIA RILKE, *Letters to a Young Poet*

acknowledgements.

Herman Daniel Farrell III,
Mary Bolin-Reece, and Geraldine Maschio
for their support during the writing of this play.

Corey Waite Arnold, Shayla Lawson,
Allen McDaniel, Timothy Ryan Olson,
Carolyn Sesbeau, John Townsend,
and Eric Vosmeier for their suggestions
and conversations.

Phi Alpha Gamma received its world premiere on July 31, 2008, at the University of Minnesota's Rarig Center Xperimental Theatre, as part of the Minnesota Fringe Festival. It was performed by Dan Bernitt.

The play was developed with the support of a research and creativity grant from the University of Kentucky and a fellowship from the Gaines Center for the Humanities.

characters.
(in order of speaking)

AARON, 21.

PATRICK, 21.

DAVID, 20.

JACOB, 20.

a note on performance.

Phi Alpha Gamma was written to be performed by one actor. Character changes should be made with subtle theatricality to maintain the script's quick pace.

The script in this book contains hard paragraph breaks and scripted pauses. Hard breaks are used for general brief pauses in speaking, as well as for clarity in reading. Scripted pauses are included for breaks with more intention.

parados.

Lights up on a table and stool. This set remains stationary throughout the play; only differences in lighting will establish spaces.

A brother walks into the space: he's been sweating, panting. He wears a t-shirt and gym shorts.

He paces.

On the table he writes on a piece of paper. He writes for several moments. It is difficult: words he's finally found, words that summon lurking demons.

He scrawls something, then folds the paper, hides it.

prologue.

(A prison cell.)

AARON

Man, you ever had one of those times in your life where you just don't know why you did something? You drive home and forget to pick up your brother. You make coffee after dinner, but start the regular blend instead of decaf. You leave the screen door open at night, and the rain soaks the carpet; the smell stays. A joke you thought was funny doesn't deliver the same punch with new friends. Usually you can brush it off: apologize to your brother; pour the coffee down the drain; Febreze. An' all's new.

But whaddaya do with the heavier stuff? I mean, you can toss somethin' into a river, the water takes it downstream, but you're still left standing on the bank, still left with the river. You can toss off everything you've ever owned, but — you still have your hands. You gettin' this, buddy?

episode.

PATRICK

PATRICK

(*Chanting:*)

Born proud raised proud who the hell are we?!
Phi Alpha Gamma best men best fraternity! Born
proud raised proud who the hell are we?!

(*He pauses for an answer. None. He speaks more
directly to the audience.*)

Come on, rushes, you all should know this. Say
it with me. Try it again: "Phi Alpha Gamma, best
men best fraternity." This should be in your bones
by now! "Born proud raised proud who the hell
are we?!"

(*Waits:*)

Yes. Finally. Thank you. A little louder next time.

This is the biggest pledge class we've had in the
past two years. And, on behalf of the fraternity,

I welcome each and every one of you to the brotherhood. I think I met all of you guys during rush week, but in case you've forgotten me, my name is Patrick McKenzie. I'm a poli-sci junior, and I am president of the chapter. I also serve on IFC – the interfraternity council – so if you happen to let your grades slip or ya do somethin' stupid, you'll be answerin' to me. But, y'know, I'm not all into yelling at guys before they've done shit wrong – it's not the tone we wanna set. The brothers here, we picked you for the kinds of men we saw during rush week, and we think you all are the kinda guys we wanna spend our time with. Y'know, share our home with. So until ya fuck up —

(*He chuckles.*)

Which ya won't, but – 'til ya fuck up – welcome. Welcome home.

DAVID

One night, a bunch of the guys were hanging out in the living room. One of them mentioned how Patrick's speech at the beginning of the year really touched him. He said something like "You know, I've never really been part of a group that didn't yell at me as soon as I joined. Patrick really made me feel welcomed." I guess he had never been to Bible camp before; I did that all the time growing up. But I can imagine, from talking to other guys at camp, that, y'know, guys get picked on a lot for being guys. Like they're automatically going to cause problems when together. Then another guy piped up – and he said "You know why he" – Patrick – "why he said that, right?" The bit about messing up, doing something wrong that could look bad on our group. He started talking about Aaron.

Most of the guys hadn't even heard of what happened. Guess the rumors have kinda died down, thank the Lord. Well, this new guy said: "Yeah, man, there was a gay bashing that happened. One of the dudes in the fraternity beat up some homosexual" — well, he said 'faggot,' not 'homosexual;' then he mentioned that Aaron's in prison now. I must've looked up from reading, because the guy talking about it said, "Hey David, did you know the guy?" I put my Bible down and said, "Yes. Yes, we were in the same pledge class." He asked what he was like, and I said Aaron was a good person; he just did a really terrible thing. They kept prodding me for details. Now, I can understand their curiosity, but — it's something we don't like to discuss.

(*Pause.*)

It was a very trying time for all of us in the fraternity. Some of the homosexual groups on campus were targeting us, saying that we caused it to happen. But we – well, mostly it was Patrick, he was a freshman at the time – but we issued a very formal statement, saying that it was one member of our group who attacked the man in the park – it should not represent all of us. We do not condone violence.

But the homosexual groups. They're vicious. I don't know who organizes them together, but they put together a candlelight vigil for the guy Aaron attacked. He didn't even die! He only got his arm twisted or something. But, yes, they held a vigil for a young man who was looking for some anonymous homosexual casual sex at night in a public park. It's really disturbing. They turn something so ugly into something worthy of honor. They turn the potential for disease into beauty. And in turn hurt how we look, guys who had nothing to do with it. It's so incredibly offensive an-and repulsive.

Thank the Lord we had – have – Patrick in our group. He does absolute wonders. He is so beautifully eloquent. Without fail, he motivates all of us to do better, to be better. He pulled this group through a very tough time.

JACOB

Patrick's been buggin' me 'bout my grades since freshman year. Hell, even when he ain't wasn't even president or nothing. For, like, two years it's all about English or math or chemistry or – just e'rythin'. Says that we gotta keep up our average GPA – "can't have any dead weight." Guess that's what I am: dead weight. I mean, he means it all nice, but it still kinda stings. Like, I'm not w— I dunno.

Anyway, he keeps setting up little tutorin' sessions for me. I'm finally gettin' the hang a' things; midterm's coming up, and I got this killer exam in chemistry. Like, I'm majorin' in chemistry – I like it good enough, but it's always real bad hard.

But, y'know, Patrick asked me, y'know, "hey, why doncha ask Louis if he'd help ya with chem stuff?" Lou's my little brother in the fraternity. He's a shy kinda guy – usually stays in his room. Don't bother no one. Nice guy, but real quiet. Just stays in 'is room. Well, he's been helpin' me with my chem stuff recently. He explains it real good – always gots some kinda easy way for me to remember things.

So we're on this section about sorption and desorption. Like, I can understand sorption: you know, like, materials of different states – gas, liquid, solid – gettin' 'corp'rated together, molecules bondin'. But desorption just confuses me. So Louis is trying to explain it all to me. And the entire time he's a-tellin' me this, just explaining this to me, he's all, like, "now stay with me, stay with me" – like I was leavin' him or somethin'. I'm not understandin'. I just don't know how some kinda chemical can be removed from another once they done been bonded. And I asks Lou this, and he says, "well, yeah, they don't just stop. If they bond, they don't separate on they own. There's gotta be a catalyst of some sort."

He's just rattlin' off this chemistry stuff, like it's his life story or something. And I'm gettin' near close to understandin', and he asks me – "do you know how I know this?" – an' I say, "cuz y'read the damn book so many times?"

(*Slight chuckle.*)

He looks kinda hurt when I say that. Almost scared like. An' I'm like, "Man, it was a joke." An' he looks away, starts mumblin' something. So I ask 'im if'll speak up. He looks at me, starts stutterin' a bit. And I'm, like, "man, you okay? Y'need some water?" He shakes his head, still real scared like. And I'm, like, Lou, man. Breathe. Y'scarin' me somethin' bad. An' he does. Real slow. He's gettin' ready to speak and he's, like, "Yeah, haha, you're right. It's the book. I read it all the time."

DAVID

I spend most of my free time in the living room, studying Scripture. It makes me feel centered, like I have a purpose whenever I have the chance to speak. It, too, gets me through tough times. Well, the guys kept asking me questions about Aaron. Asked me if anyone still keeps in touch with him.

And I tell them that I send him letters. You know, he must be awfully alone and scared. At 19, he was sentenced to serve time in prison. Nineteen! So I send him verses from the Bible, verses of hope, of salvation, of caring and truth. I think that he's in an extremely tough situation, even though he willingly committed an act that put him there – don't get me wrong – but he's young.

I try to offer him a chance to be saved. I would like nothing more, nothing would be more beautiful than to have him be born again while in prison. Nothing would bring me more joy than to know that, no matter what, he is safe in Jesus' arms. I say this to the guys, and they all nod. You can see the Lord at work in moments like these. Moments when a conversation that seemed geared on gossip turns into one of truth seeking. Moments when people truly bond – where a community is born.

JACOB

By this time I'm not sure if Lou's just makin' fun of me or what, so I'm like, "C'mon, man. I was joking. Really, like, tell me how ya know this." Jus' bein' polite or somethin'. So he starts tellin' me this story. He starts an' says, "Well, Jacob. Whew. Um, so r-remember when, last spring, I disappeared for a coupla days? The flu I had?" And I'm, like, yeah – you gettin' like this to tell me about havin' the flu? And he puts his hand up, like tellin' me to shut up. So I do. This little man's gettin' pretty fierce, like this new person in fronta me. He says that they, at the hospital, they had him drink a charcoal mixture. Now I'd never heard of charcoal fixin' flu symptoms – I mean, if it did I'd be eatin' right outta them barbeque pits whenever my throat would starta tickle! – but, y'know, I wasn't gonna interrupt him again. Then he says, "Man, Jacob, I've never told anyone this before, but, um ... I didn't have the flu." And I'm, like, okay, so what happened – and what's this gotta do with chemistry? An' he says, "Aspirin." He says: "I took a whole bottle of pain killers."

(*Pause.*)

And I'm, like, getting angry at him now. Angry, like, man, why'd the hell y'do that? My Memay always told me to jus' respect your body cuz it's the only thing you ever gonna own. But he starts to get scared again, so I say to myself, like, Jacob, man, calm down – don't get angry at 'im. Lou's gettin' this worried look. So I say, "Louis, man, if there's somethin' wrong, you can tell me about it. I mean, I might not be able to help ya, but David's real good at findin' the right scriptures, and I can listen. But, man, why did you do that? Are you okay?" He pauses. He swallows hard. And he just says it: "Man, I think I'm gay."

PATRICK

That is something you do not do. These guys stumble into the house, completely fucked up out of their minds. Wasted and shit. We're, what — a month or so into having the new brothers in the house, and someone fucks up now. You could see he was blazed. Okay, it was John and Peter; Peter was holding John up, a little drunk himself, and John was just bleedin' and angry as fuck. This was Saturday night. And Peter and John come stumbling into the house – start knocking over shit. John's got a cut above his right eye, and Peter's got his shirt off, twisted into knots and blotting at John's face. And John's trying to fight him off, saying "yo-yo-yo, I'm fine." The moment John starts walking away, he starts crashing into walls again. I hear this shit from a room over — Pete says "Dude, I can't believe you knocked that guy out!"

So I get up and go into the foyer, where they are, and John's down on the ground, shit-eatin' grin, saying "Huh-huh, yeah, I got him good, yeah." And the kid's wearing a t-shirt with the letters. Brand-new guy, like eighteen, from a small town, thinkin' he owns the world or some shit like that. And I look at him, and I'm like "Didja have a good night?" They see me, and they're, like, "Oh shit." And I'm, like, "Y'damn right. What's going on?" They're all like "oh, nothing," trying to cover it up. But I look at John, and I say, "John – you're bleeding from your face, your clothes are — messed up. You didn't knock out a bush."

So they start tryin' to impress me with some story. Went to a house party, keg beer, fighting over some girl, lame shit like that – some guy in another fraternity started hitting on a girl John was flirting with. So, the beer in them, they started to trash talk. Obvious John can't hold his drink for shit, cuz he threw the first punch. And the entire time they're telling me this lame-ass story, I'm thinking: "This is what you do on a Saturday night? Get so drunk you can't think straight, and pick a fight while wearing your letters." They're talking about the incident, making it sound all like a fierce battle, and I say to them, "Yeah, guys, I know. I've been there. I've had some stupid drunken times, and, yeah, I've been in fights, too. That can be all well and good, all fun. But, guys, we've got a problem here. You all are going around in our letters picking your fights? Not cool. I don't care if it's some fraternity-versus-fraternity scenario – you're still out there making an impression on us. And it looks like you lost the fight, so imagine what folks think of you now. Grow up, kid."

They got quiet. Nodded. And I say, "We're gonna talk about this in our next chapter meeting – what to and what not to do while wearing your letters. It seems like I haven't made myself clear." They shut up. Walked upstairs, went to bed. Never seen someone sober up so quickly.

Just pisses me off that these guys think they're independent of the group, but still need the group to have any clout. Surprise: we've expelled guys who've harmed our good name. Sometimes you just got to remove the dead weight.

JACOB

I look at Lou. His eyes just starin' at me. And I see his face turning white, and it looks like he's startin' to panic – and I realize I ain't said nothin' yet. I mean, whaddaya say when your little brother tells ya he's gay? "What?" I was still mad that 'e done tried to kill hisself. But I just look at him an' I tell 'im: man, you're all right. Man, ya still my brother. You bein' gay ain't gon' change that. Just promise me: you ain't gonna try to kill yourself again. And he just sighs – this big ol' — (*Relief.*)

An' he says, "Yeah. Yeah!" He looked like everythin' in 'is life just flipped. So I say, "Hey, um, can we get back to this chem stuff?" And he just laughs, an' says yeah.

(*Slight laugh.*)

Feels like I finally got an answer right.

(*Pause.*)

Right then, there was a knock on the door. Patrick comes inside. Says it's about time for the chapter meeting; said he was checkin' the rooms to get people downstairs. He heads out, and Lou looks at me and says: "Do you think he heard?" And I'm, like, heard what? "Um, us talking." And I'm, like, I doubt it. Even if he did, so what? It's not that big of a deal, man. There are good guys here. Don't have much to worry about. He nods, says yeah. I pat him on the back and tell him "C'mon, bro, we should go."

stasimon.

(From prison.)

AARON

Shooting the last hoop, I caught your air ball,
dribbled it, and asked if you wanted to play another
game. You said sure. You said alright. Didn't
know I didn't mean basketball. I said follow me,
we walked on the sidewalk, walked on the grass, on
the dew, the twigs snapped beneath our feet. You
asked a question: where and when and how and
what and why. I said shhh, said listen, I'll show
you something new. Said my brother taught me
this – now I'll teach you.

Do you remember? Do you?

Do not make noise. Do not make a sound. Do not
ask. Do not question. Only look and search and
find. There – over there. First you search for the
people alone, people waiting for someone, someone

indefinite. Then you look for poses, glances at passersby. Look for what he has or doesn't have: if food, then there's money; if clothes nicer than yours, then there's money. Watch for one – wait for a second. Wait for their glances, how they pass on the sidewalk, the pause followed by a headturn – pay attention to where they both end up walking together. Do all this, watch this unfold – stay hidden.

If alone, sneak to the bushes where they lay. If in a group, go separately and surround them. Sneak up quietly. With stealth and silence. Heart racing as you sneak up on them? Just remember: the first time is always the hardest. Remember: face away from light. Remember: you're in control. Listen close for their fumbling. Snap a twig, snap it loud and definite. Just once. Stay still for them to quiet down again, until they become a whisper.

If they're standing, wait for another. If they're kneeling, wait until they start fucking. If they're naked or pantless, go for their clothes and throw them into light. No naked man will chase you.

Now your gut might wrench. It's your first time; it will pass. Wait for the rhythm of their pounding to match the rhythm of your heart's thumps – then it's time to break.

Rustle the branches with all your might, the wood shaking in your fist, the leaves shattering stillness. Holler and laugh. Mock and moan. Scream and wail and shout. Keep your eyes locked; let your tongue rip loose. Say their names; say all their names. Ready your feet and start to chase. But leave it at that: the chase. Only a chase.

It was all a game until one tripped and presented an opportunity for a lesson. We circle and taunt. He bellows and lies. The chanting and recanting. The pushing and falling. Cause. Effect. Like the hip bone's connected to the leg bone. Arm bone and the shoulder bone dislocated by my hand. His mouth thunders as my own howls. Two bodies meet under the same moon. Do you remember?

Do you remember shouting for me to take his shit and leave? Do you remember asking me if we were done yet? Do you remember asking me again and again, the pleading deepening each time? Do you?

The drive back to the house: in my car swerving and speeding away from the scene, calm coming only in red lights. I thought they won't catch us, catch me. Next day waking up to a knock on our bedroom door. People were here to see me: my car, my license plate, the letters on my back window. In a flash the uniforms and badges swerve from hello-my-name-is to you-better-come-with-us. Hands on my wrists and faces of people as the cops escorted me out. In questioning I saved you. They said there were two, "there were two people," but I said, "No, no, maybe I beat him so hard he saw double." My last joke.

A blur these moments to now: zero to 60, 80, 90 and faster before I knew I could've braked. Now pen and paper and these letters I write, before that nothing in the cell, before that not even in a cell, before that the judge and his gavel and a jury of my peers, before that just a series of questions. Before that I wasn't a light sleeper. Now I am forever awakened by crashes, by light, by the pound of wood against wood. Fate decided by a pounding gavel.

episode.

Seeing that all members are present, I call this meeting to order. Tonight's agenda consists only of a review of proper display of our symbols – the Greek letters – and, if we have a committee update regarding the formal, we can hear from them now. Those opposed to this agenda, say aye.

(*Beat.*)

Agenda approved. Anything from the committee regarding the formal?

(*Silence.*)

Nothing.

Alright, it looks like it'll be a short meeting. I just wanna treat this like a normal conversation, so, I move to suspend the rules of a standard meeting. David, thank you for seconding. All opposed, say aye. Alright – rules suspended. So, Greek letters. There was an incident the other night of a brother wearing his letters at a party. He drank too much, and this young man ended up getting into a fight with a brother from another fraternity. Names are unimportant, but this brother put the fraternity's name and image on the line. Granted, yes, it was a silly fight they had, but it's just something you don't do.

So, there are two really easy rules when it comes to letters. One: only brothers can wear the letters. No girlfriends. No family. Just brothers. And two: do not do anything unbecoming of the fraternity while wearing your letters. Sororities are incredibly strict about this, especially with drinking. But in the fraternity, we aren't too strict. The main guideline for this is: if you have to ask, then take off your letters. If you even think it might look bad on the group, don't do it. So, guys, if you're out drinking – which you're technically not supposed to do until you're 21, but whatever – a couple beers is fine, y'know, it's social. But if you can't stop after a couple drinks, then take off your letters and wear something else. Simple, all right?

Now, yes, sometimes fights break out between fraternities. Last year there was this fight between the Chis and the Sigs. Huge fuckin' brawl. Everyone in both those fraternities went out and busted ass. War. Two guys who started it just started goin' at it, an' then their brothers joined in. S'whatcha do for a brother. But yeah, people got a little roughed up; that shit comes with the territory. S'different that goin' somewhere and pickin' a fight.

(*Pause.*)

The reason I say it is because of the incident a few years ago with a member of our fraternity being involved in an attack on a gay guy. I've heard a few of you guys talking about this stuff. Just wanna clear it all up. The cops came here to the house, arrested him, made a ridiculously huge scene, and it's plagued us since. Few guys wanted to pledge the following year because of the name of the house. But things are slowly getting back to normal. Another bad incident, and we're fucked. And that is not going to happen. Right? I will not allow any of you to act in a way that makes the rest of us look bad. I will not.

I mean, you can't just go around kicking people's asses, even if they are a fag. Like, when we were picking the guys this year – I'll say it – there was this really faggy guy who rushed. I remember some guys saying that they'd run that faggot out of the house if he tried anything. We'd fuckin' throw him out the window. But you can't just attack anyone like that. And so when this brother, Aaron, got his ass caught, it was decided – a done deal. You can't get in trouble like that; we don't want the police knocking on our front door with any warrants or shit. And with these houses as close as they are, people are gonna notice.

So we did what we hadda do: we told everyone flat out we aren't violent. Like, we'll talk about kickin' ass, but we're real careful about actually doing that shit. It's different than going into a park and attacking someone, or being in a joke of a fight between fraternities. You just don't do something that stupid.

JACOB

As Patrick said alla this, I sat there thinking back on alla times he's said stuff like this: saying gay jokes, saying hateful things. And how everyone's really agreein' with him on it all. Laughin'. Louis was sittin' next to me, his hands folded in his lap, prayerfully almost. An' I'm thinking, how does he feel 'bout this? I'm gettin' nervous for him just sitting next to him, but he just seems so calm. I think maybe he's gotten used to it by now, maybe he plays along.

Lou don't talk much to begin with, and not many people seem to know 'im, really — but then he says right to the group — "You all act like you're innocent." Everyone just turns their head and stares at 'im. And he says, "Guys, I know how homophobic you all are – tell me how this is not also violent." Something so to-the-point, coming from this small guy. I didn't even know he done had it in him.

PATRICK

I'm a little taken aback by Louis. He rarely says anything; this is the time he's making a statement?

So I say to him: "Hey, Lou, ya got some fag friends we don't know about? I'm just talkin' about letters, dude. Why are you so defensive?" And he answers: "Because that fag you talk about is me."
Point blank. Bam.

Then there's this death silence. Like, hell, I don't even know how to describe it. A silence you can't — a silence you can't shake from yourself. Just this feeling like — oh shit, this guy's been with us for years. We've been in the showers together. We've all joked and bonded and this entire time he could be — thinking of us. And him. Like, doin' gay shit.

And — it was like a bomb had gone off. None of us knew where it was coming from. Like — I don't even know. The last thing you'd ever expect in our house. And, damn — guys are gettin' angry. How did this happen? How did this guy get into our group? And then someone was, like, "Dude. What the fu-u-uck?" What all of us were thinkin'. And we all start laughing, out of this — (*Shivers.*)

While I'm laughing I'm actually – freakin' out

a little bit. Here's another thing I have to worry about: another strike against us. Not only are we the violent group that attacks gay people, but now we're the gay fraternity? I know that's exactly how people will spin it. I know. People will latch onto that like — they won't let it go. And while people are reacting, I'm thinking of a solution. How are we going to deal with this?

DAVID

I can see already – this will deeply affect us. A homosexual around us, in our safety zone. I can sense this in the room: the young men looking at each other's reactions – all of them laughing by this point. Some of them angry. And here: this small young man, Louis. Even the tiniest can cause the greatest of impacts.

I know Patrick said that the rules are dismissed at this point, but we definitely need some order. I made a motion to let us work through this issue. I kindly asked Louis to leave – if only for a little bit, from the meeting room. And he begins to get incredibly defensive: "Why do I have to leave? I'm a brother here. I am part of this group, too!" And people are shouting – one guy says, "well, y'aren't now." I say to Louis – Louis, my brother, the reason I ask you to leave is not because you are a homosexual or because we don't want you here. Yes, absolutely, you are a brother in our fraternity, but I think it is in your best interest for us to deal with this privately. Yes, I understand that this involves you – this is entirely about you. But I feel that I can help provide some guidance to the group. I tell him – and I am forthright in saying this, I am – it is my intention to sort through the feelings of the group. I feel I can be a mediator in this setting. Just allow me this.

PATRICK

David had talked to him for a little bit and convinced the guy to leave. Louis just stood up, real pissed, and he marched out of the room. Threw open the door, slammed it shut.

JACOB

I sat in my seat, stunned. Something so quick. Here. Now. One of them moments when you know everything here out will be different. Louis's seat next to me – empty, not even pushed in. But when that door slammed, it's like the first word on everyone's mind was "faggot."

stasimon.

(From prison.)

AARON

The door slams shut, and I'm in a cell.

The door slams shut, and I'm in a cafeteria.

The door slams shut, and I'm stuck.

My cell mate is from Milwaukee. People call him King. King. First-degree murder. He spends his time exercising. He has more bulk than I could ever have. His arms are — as thick as my head. He eyes me. He doesn't stop. I sit still on my bunk. He lets me sleep on the top.

He watches me around the other prisoners. I try to watch my back. I keep to myself most of the time. I do what I need to do. I try to sleep with the noise and the light. I try to forget.

Some of the other men here try to gang up on me. They call me boy. They call me cunt. They say, "I bet you'd be real nice." When one pushed me against the wall in the shower, King knocked him away. I might be over six feet tall, but I —

Back in our cells – late at night, or so I think – King nudges my bunk. "Yo. Aaron." Yeah, King? "Aaron, get down here, man." I hop off the bunk, and King's sitting on his bed. "Man, if you wanna survive in here, you're gonna need some help." He tells me about things he's heard other guys say. Plans to attack me, to choke me in the shower, force me to — They all think it's a great joke that I attacked some faggot, so now they want to turn me into one. Either that, or they want me dead. Either way I'm fucked.

King says: "You'll be my punk." Your punk? "I'm making you a deal, man." I don't know the terms, so — "I make sure you don't get hurt and no one fucks with you. You just do what I tell you." I ask him like what? He gets up from his bunk and says for me to lie down. "Lie down and shut up." I lie down, facing my bunk, King comes and flips me over. He rips down my pants, I try to stop him, he grips my wrist firm and tightens his hand. Our eyes meet: "I'll make sure you're safe." He's rubbing himself, I know what he means, I look away.

The mattress creaks as he's pushing into me. He says get up, get on the floor, get on your knees. I kneel – ready for this to be over, maybe it'll be quick, maybe he'll let me go. Down on the floor, I see a leak from our toilet. I hear a tablespoon of water can drown you if you breathe it in, and with each thrust I'm gasping, each punch and I'm pulling my lips to water, and when I taste slime or mold or piss or dirt I know I'm not breathing it in and I know it's not working and my face is hot and my ass burns and I can't take my mind off it. I'm clawing and he's bucking and I think he knows what I'm trying to do cuz my shoulder's in his grip, the calluses of his fingers on my skin. My eyes see nothing but from a distance the water dripping in a pool.

For a moment I see you and me behind the bushes in the park, right before the faggots came. If you get them when they're about cum, my brother once told me, that's the best time. That's all they worry about, no worries other than keeping hard.

King has his thick arm wrapped around my torso, his grip pinching my underarm. I'm the twig breaking in a hand, the noise triggering downfall. His other hand covers my mouth: my tears on his rough finger. He whispers in my ear: "This will make you safe, punk." He presses his sweaty cheek against my temple with one final throbbing jerk.

episode.

JACOB

They was just a buncha jerks to make Louis leave like that. Right when the door shut, Patrick says: "On the topic of letters, that is also something you don't do while wearing our name." An' everyone lets out this sigh of relief, like thank God that's over, thank God we're free. An' usu'ly I'm real quiet at these meetin's, not really much I gotta say. Just like being around my brothers, y'know. An' I just say to 'em: "S'real mean'a ya to treat'm like he's some kinda outsider."

PATRICK

Jacob, Lou's always been distant from us. Like, hanging out in his room, drinking alone in there. We invite him to do shit with us, and it's hard as hell to even get him to these weekly meetings. He makes himself the outsider, buddy.

I guess now he's just been beating off to the thought of us. For a while, y'know, after he got sick last year, I thought he was gonna move out, but I guess he couldn't stand to be away from us – nothing to jerk off to, I guess.

It's so sick, man. Makes me — (*Shudders.*) I bet that's what he does.

DAVID

Brothers, we have a serious issue here. I think we need to discuss this like rational men. Louis has shared a very personal thing with us. We are not unaccustomed to brothers sharing personal secrets. This is nothing unusual. I feel that we should let this be a bonding moment for us all. A moment for us all to share our feelings with the group. Take a moment to strengthen our fellowship.

Friends, you may have heard repeatedly the scriptures declaring homosexuality a sin and that those who commit it shall surely be put to death.

That doesn't mean we kill Louis. Friends, remember Jesus' phrase: "Judge not lest you be judged." And anyway, if you are going to boast the rules of Leviticus, you must follow them all. So if you have eaten a cheeseburger or had your hair cut, then you, too, have a ticket to damnation. Friends, Leviticus is not the issue. And I resent any notion from you to tout these passages. It is disrespectful of my beliefs and of the Word of God to pick and choose outdated passages like that.

But we must look at broader, more modern passages. 1 Corinthians, chapter 5. The Apostle Paul writes of sexual immorality – which I think Louis is on a similar path: "Shouldn't you rather have been filled with grief and have put out of your fellowship the man who did this?" And later: "Don't you know that a little yeast works through the whole batch of dough? Get rid of the old yeast that you may be a new batch without yeast – as you really are. For Christ, our Passover lamb, has been sacrificed. Therefore let us keep the Festival —" in this case, our fraternity "— not with the old yeast, the yeast of malice and wickedness, but with bread without yeast, the bread of sincerity and truth." And he closes that section, chapter 5 verse 11, with "you must not associate with anyone who calls himself a brother but is sexually immoral ... With such a man do not even eat."

As I say all of this, Jacob – I adore this guy: he knows Scripture better than a lot of folks, s'what makes debate so good with him – he comes back with another verse. 1 John 2:10: "Whoever loves his brother lives in the light." Then he skips a bit to the next chapter, 3:10: "Anyone who does not do what is right is not a child of God, nor is anyone who does not love his brother."

(*Pause.*)

You could hear the Angels at work in our chapter room. Everyone rapt with divine attention at how our conversation will unfold. Rapt with an innate desire for The Truth.

I let that phrase linger. Not a passage people often select. I let that feeling linger – let the brothers contemplate it. And then I ask the group: would you rather be robbed of your possessions by a burglar in the night, or live in a home haunted by spirits?

This is not a rhetorical question.

(*He speaks more directly to the audience.*)

Which would you choose: robbed or haunted? Peter, this new brother, said he'd rather have the spirits. And I asked him why he said that. He kinda shrugged. So I say, "Peter — and all brothers — when a burglar comes into your home, he wants your belongings, your possessions – all your DVDs, CDs, iPod, computer. You call the police, file a report, maybe your stuff'll be found, maybe you have insurance to pay for replacements. You buy new locks, safeguard your home – in time all will be well again.

"But when a demon enters your home, no deadbolt can keep it away. Somehow it got inside. And this spirit doesn't want any of your belongings; what's a demon going to do with an iPod?

(*He teeters on the edge of the performing space.*)

No, brothers, the only thing a demon wants – is you."

Like yeast in the dough. Like a demon in our home. I am very concerned with how this new revelation about Louis will affect our group. Look at us now – how uneasy everyone is with this intrusion. There is a shift in the power within our group – we've been robbed of it because of a single incident. Robbed of a delicate intangible.

(*He returns to the scene.*)

Brothers, I care for Louis. I do. He is our brother, yes. But I, too, care deeply this brotherhood, which includes all the brothers. I am more than willing to counsel Louis and help him overcome this. I am, however, — and I can sense this from others — uncomfortable with him being here. I do not take lightly this scenario. This task.

And I say to Jacob, allow us to wrestle with what the text says. I say to him, "Yes, brother is singular in that passage. But to include one at the expense of the whole is a dangerous situation of which Paul speaks, and one which we – the big brothers, almost fathers, in this fraternity – have experienced before. I encourage you to look deeper in that same passage

you cited, Jacob. 1 John. Chapter 3, verses 12-14.
Young men, listen to Jacob read this."

JACOB

"I write to you, dear children,
because your sins have been forgiven
on account of his name.
I write to you, fathers,
because you have known him
who is from the beginning.
I write to you, young men,
because you have overcome the evil one.

 (*Beat.*)

"I write to you, dear children,
because you have known the Father.
I write to you, fathers,
because you have known him
who is from the beginning.
I write to you, young men,
because you are strong,
and the word of God lives in you,
and you've overcome the evil one."

 (*Pause.*)

When I finish readin' I look over at David. He nods, smilin' like I gave'm 'is answer.

stasimon.

(From prison.)

AARON

Here they trick you into doing the wrong thing. Here they lie to you as a joke, then punish you for not following the rules. A loop of lies and uncertainty: I can't will myself to sleep, can't will myself awake, can't discern between being dead or alive. I test all my senses to make sure I'm alive. When I gag or wince, I know I'm still alive. When I see a guard acknowledge what's happening and do nothing to stop it, I know I'm still here. When I — when King pushes to the back of my mouth until all I can do to keep safe is reason myself away from choking — I know I'm alive.

I sit next to King at meals. No one messes with me. No one talks to me, not even King. To him — I'm a toy tighter than a hand. To others, a sea of lost boys and men — I'm just another sad face.

Eating the same shit.

An apple sits on my tray. I look at the apple. I know it's an apple. Oh, wow, apple. But something in me tells me that that, too, is a lie. It's hard to explain, but in here truth is never solid. At the table I start breathing quick, I have to reassure myself that everything's okay. But eventually all these self-assurances turn to lies, and I'm stuck in a loop of terror. What else will soon be false? Is it just a matter of time before King gets tired? Is it?

I dreamed about you last night. I was in our dorm room. I heard this rumbling from behind the closet door. Going to check it out, the door flew open and you stood naked with your hands clenched over your eyes. I call your name; you don't answer. I call again, and you look up – a quick jerk, a flash: a rectangle around your eyes bleeds, flesh ripped, slashed, brutally cut. Your eyes butchered. You made something of a war cry, a cry held back for so long before finally emerging. You try to focus your blinded, bloody pupils on me. All I can focus on is the darkness of your pupil surrounded by red. Blood circling down a drain. Life dripping away.

I slam shut the door. But with that slam, I find there are now no windows or doors leading out. No escape. Nothing to do but sit on my bed and wait until you throw open the door. I'm an animal readying for a drink from the river, unaware of the crocodile slowly circling.

I jerk myself awake. I throw my arm to turn on my bedside lamp, but hit the concrete wall instead: I'm still in the cell. The light from the hall outside the cell streams in. I breathe, gasp hard, suck in air to try to vent out the sounds of the dream. I try not to blink because the terror returns: bloody eyes, your scowl, your fingers ready to strangle.

I wish I could say my dreams were filled with goofy shit like "and then you gave me an ice cream cone while wearing Mickey Mouse ears." The way dreams work now: things like that do occur, but the joy belongs to the wind. Ice cream melts, the cone crumbles, the mouse ears turn to snakeheads.

My back pops as King kicks his heavy foot against my mattress. "Yo, punk, get your bitch-ass cunt down here. I'm waiting."

And I do. I do. This is my only salvation. The only way to make sure I'm still alive. Have you ever seen a fox with a rabbit in its mouth? Have you ever seen how the rabbit disconnects, how it dies right before the jaw snaps shut? I wish I were a rabbit.

I wonder if any Bible quotes explain this. Is this the Lord protecting me? I wonder what I'll end up in Hell for: attacking some faggot or getting fucked in the ass so I don't get killed. Is Hell like this? Are you glad I saved you from it? Are you glad I thought you didn't have the words to save yourself?

Are you even there?

episode.

PATRICK

God and spirituality are powerful. Thank you for sharing His words with us, David – for providing clarity in such a tough moment for us all.

JACOB

And I say: Just hold it. Hold it, David, you said you can't pick an' choose what the Bible has to say. You forgot some words in that passage from Paul. Doesn't it say the same thing about people who are drunk or greedy or liars?

PATRICK

What are you trying to say by this, Jacob?

(*Beat.*)

You talkin' about drinking? If you're saying because we drink, we're ruining our brotherhood, that's stupid. I think David will agree with this as well. For us, drinking is a social thing – we don't do it to disconnect, we don't drink specifically to get drunk; right, guys? No, for us it's — time to bond. We have a beer, and we get to know one another. Now being a faggot – that's a helluva lot different. I mean, yeah, fags might really get to know each other, but — we don't need a dick in our ass in order to relate.

Jacob, I apologize that the situation in which you find yourself causes you any duress. I know that with your limited background, you find attacking those sorting through a tough matter like this the only option. I hope that you look back on whatever you say or do tonight with satisfaction and peace.

I know you're not stupid, Jacob. You can figure out what all this means. It's like the yeast-in-the-dough, throw-away-the-bread stuff. I'm sure you know how yeast works. After all, you're the chemist; I'm not.

JACOB

An' I'm gettin' so f'ustrated, man. I don't know

why Patrick — I dunno, maybe he thinks that I'm — I just don't even know whatta say. And I just say to them: "Man, I'm just sayin' that there's —" And Patrick interrupts me and I just get so mad, and I yell: "Let me finish. Let me finish talkin', Patrick, please. There is more goin' on in Louis's life than you know. Pro'ly more stuff in 'is life than you ever hadda cover up. Man, maybe David can counsel him or somethin', but —

PATRICK

Jacob. What do you care about more? Huh? Our brotherhood or some guy who doesn't even participate with us? He doesn't even come to many of the events — that's grounds for expulsion! If he doesn't want to be with us, then I say 'get out!' Either you're with the brothers, or you're not. You care about us or you don't. Obvious he doesn't care. We try. We do. But he's in his room all the time, probably whackin' off to the thought of us —

(*Laughs to himself.*)

— Gross. Jacob, you care about someone who does that? Dude.

Jacob, we are here as brothers to share the joy of fraternity. Do you mean to say that you instead support sin? Jacob, are you truly willing to support the thing that tears apart our brotherhood over the brotherhood itself.

JACOB

An' as he says this, I'm startin' to realize how, just, how they – I cannot even understand why they say these things. An' I just throw up my arms – thinkin' they'll bring Louis back in an' throw all this crap on 'im. An' I'm just thinkin', y'know, alright, I'll talk to 'im later after alla this settles. Jus' let 'im know that I don't care if he's gay. That he's still my brother. But yeah, just throw my hands up: "Enough. I'm through with this."

They bring Lou back in. Starts goin' off, sayin', "Just let me talk to you all about this. You all treat me like I'm some disease."

DAVID

Louis, this is difficult for us, too. We've never had to deal with this before. But I think the Bible is very clear about this issue.

(*Beat.*)

No, I'm not condemning you, Louis. Stop with that. It's offensive; you're limiting this discussion by getting so defensive. Hear us out.

(*Beat.*)

Like I said, the Bible is very clear on this issue. While your sexuality is an issue, it is not the entire complex problem. As you may have noticed, your disclosure has caused a rift in our — let me finish, Louis. Louis, please, let me finish — what you have disclosed to us has caused a rift in our brotherhood. It is my position, and like with Paul's letters to the Corinthians, we should reconsider your situation with this house.

(*Beat.*)

Yes, you do live here; Louis, it is our home, too. I know I am not the one to make this decision, but — Louis, it is my fear that this will only cause further disruption in our living situation. Please try to understand this.

PATRICK

Lou, we picked ya because we liked ya. We did. We do like you. It is not the fact that you're a homosexual that leaves you in question. Louis, you hardly ever attend important events with the fraternity. It's hard enough trying to get you out of your room.

Louis, I was gonna let this slide, but the number of meetings and events you've missed is grounds for expulsion. If you don't wanna be a brother, then don't be. Sad to see ya go, but that looks like the only option.

JACOB

Lou. Just looks at me. His green eyes starin'. He says: "I wanna know what Jacob has to say." An' soon as he says that, one guy, this new dude, breaks the silence, an' is, like, "What, Jake, you a fag too?" And everyone starts laughin' at us, and I just yell: "I ain't got nothin' to do with this!"

The laughter dies down a bit. Lou, his eyes still set on me, says: "No, Jacob. You had everything to do with this."

I feel like I wanna just run. But I can't. Can't no more. He shrugs, says "Sadly, Jacob, that's what I thought." Walks outta the room. The door slams, and I realize I ain't said nothin'. Silent. Just silent. Again. How can I talk to him now?

DAVID

So, Jacob. What do you have to say?

(*Beat.*)

Of course, I feel safe.

(*Beat.*)

God's Word. Jacob, I hate to repeat myself so much. The Bible is clear. It has a clarity that makes everything that happens bearable. No matter what it looks like now, no matter any circumstances, we win. I have spent my whole life to see it that I get there. I refuse to be wishywashy by any means. The Bible. It's clear. Absolutely. No matter what comes up in any setting, in any environment – it is clear.

His Word came down here to Earth from Heaven above. It traveled from His World to ours. And these letters, Jacob, these letters, from Paul and the other apostles, each one is clear proof of God's love. These letters to us show us His love.

How can I enjoy Heaven if I don't let other people know this joy? I won't. I won't be able to enjoy Heaven if I think about all the people who I could have told, who I could have helped guide in the right way. In the way of the Light. That is why I speak about this so much. Because I want to share the joy I have, in my heart, with all those around me. If there are doubts – w-which there surely are not – this is my rock. My foundation. This book. Clear.

PATRICK

Huh?

(*Beat.*)

What kinda question is that, Jacob? Yeah, I'm safe.

(*Beat.*)

I don't know how I know, Jacob. For Christ's sake

— forgive me, David — I'm frustrated, alright? It's never enough, y'know. Sometimes it's not enough to simply put one foot in fronta the other, y'know, and persevere.

But, dammit, I don't know what else to do. After trying my damnedest to make sure we aren't known as 'the violent fraternity,' 'the aggressive fraternity,' 'the fraternity of attackers' — shit, Jacob, you feel like you can ask that? Do I feel safe now that Louis is gone? I don't know what else to do.

No matter what, people hate us – even if we're just a buncha regular guys, people already have bad ideas about us. That we're rapists or stupid or alcoholics or whatever. They don't know that we are better than that. They don't understand that this – these four years are our only time together, to just be guys. Seems long while we're here, but after graduation, guys, this is it. Over. Done. Finished. 'Best four years,' or whatever our dads or – anyone may say. Gone.

I just wanna make sure I can enjoy it and be myself and be with brothers in the moments when I'm not fuckin' thinking about my future, y'know. I mean, it might not be right but — all I can do. What else can I do?

(*Pause.*)

I don't know. I dunno why I joined. Hang out? I dunno. Hell, why'd you join?

JACOB

An' I told 'em, "I want that, too. Y'all know 'bout how I grew up with my Memay, and my folks weren't around. An' she'd always try to get me to get out an' be with people.

"I joined cuz I wanna build more. Now without much family, it's, like, I wanna have folks to be around, brothers to live with, people I could always have, y'know, t'just talk to. I don't really got the words to describe it, really. But— but it seems like if ya mess up, yr'out. Seems like I gotta find something else, an-an' I dunno where'dlook. Dunno – just hoping there'd be love here.

(*A long pause.*)

"I'm sorry; I can't keep sittin' here no more. I gotta go clear my head, go to bed, sleep, something."

Yeah.

Meeting adjourned.

stasimon.

(From prison.)

Hello friend.   Still haven't heard anything from
you.   Still hope you're at your address at the good
ol' fraternity.   Hope you've been getting my letters.

Nothing's really changed.   Still having nightmares
of you with lacerated eyes, still rooming with King,
still getting ass raped, still in this delightful place
for another, oh, three years. Yep, this is the life!

Y'know, there's a certain amount of comfort, safety,
in being called pet names: boy, kid, fuckboy, honey,
catcher. That last one, "catcher," makes me feel like
I'm part of a team! I called him names, too: papi,
Big Man, my poundaholic! That last one got me
a punch in the kidney, but hey, that's better than
bein' gutted in the shower, right?

I'm fooling no one, am I? Not you. I'm sure it's better out there. I'm sure that you are free to speak, talk. Be with a chick, forchrissakes. Play basketball. Shoot hoops without the competition of other guys starin' you down.

Been thinkin' a lot about the incident. How a moment of me feelin' high on power got me here. Then I got to thinkin' about my brother – how he taught me that, to attack. Guess I went into it cuz I wanted to have him think I was cool. That I could hang.

Then I started thinkin' back to why I did it. Why I pounced *that* guy, why I broke his arm and didn't even know what I did until after it snapped.

One guy in here, this black dude, I heard him talkin' about privilege. How The White Man has privilege cuz he's white. And how there's privilege with money and other shit – he was goin' on about alla this stuff. Started thinkin', like, "yeah, I got that!" Or, at least I used to. But just cuz I got some kinda leg up doesn't mean I'm all better off.

I mean, when I was attackin' that guy – maybe I was fightin' cuz I was jealous. I wanted an escape, like, from the responsibility of all that. And here are these faggots, just runnin' off to a park to get a chance to be free. I didn't want what they were doin' – but maybe I wanted what they felt. And maybe I felt like if I can't have a chance to escape, then they shouldn't either.

I know they don't deserve that. I know that doesn't excuse what I did – at all. I know now it just causes more pain in ways I never would've imagined. I know that. Now. But maybe – like, it helps me understand why I did it. This mask is all I'm allowed to wear. And it's all you're allowed to wear, too, Jacob.

Probably said too much anyway, probably too much for you to handle. Probably said too much in general. Whatever. It's all I have now. But, hey – if you get this letter, cool. I've written you enough already, don't know why this one'll get you to write me back. But, Jacob, I know you've been getting these.

I just know.

No matter what the fraternity may say, we're still brothers. Might've gotten kicked out, but I'm not done. We're not finished yet.

Sincerely,
Aaron

exodos.

(JACOB finds the letter he had drafted earlier. He unfolds it, and reads it aloud with difficulty, giving breath to the words that were once demons.)

JACOB

Dear Aaron,

I got yer letters. Don't really know exactly what it all means, but I know I can't get whatcha wrote outta my head.

Before writing this, I shot some hoops on the court right by the fraternity house. Thinkin' it felt so good out here, felt free. Chilly night air; open court, silent except for the cars way out on the interstate. Reminds me of the night we played horse. The night you beat me. The last time.

Before that, we had a fraternity meeting. Talked about a lotta stuff I never thought would come up.

Before that, I felt like I had a grasp back on things.

Before that, I put your last letter under my bed, in an envelope with the rest. Used to be I never got no mail. Things felt clearer then.

Before that, the police hauled you away. You vanished. Before that, my grades didn't slip as much.

Before that, in the fall, you introduced yourself as my big brother. I felt like you meant it. I didn't know how deep you did mean it. We started together as brothers. You said hello as you shook my hand.

Before that, all the brothers taught us our chant: "Born proud, raised proud, who the hell are we? Phi Alpha Gamma, best men, best fraternity." I used to just shout it loud with all the rest. Now I get stuck. Born proud, raised proud. Who the hell are we?

I don't know if I'll ever know the answer.

I told the guys tonight at the meeting why I joined.
I want brothers. You know this. But I said that it
feels like brotherhood's always on edge. An' now,
after tonight, I don't know if I can go on with them.
Not Patrick, not David, not even — not any of 'em.
Feels like it can all shift without no warnin'.

I know I ain't said nothing 'til now. I know I ain't
been keeping up at all. I know I've been neglecting
you. I know you deserve better than that. We both
do. Maybe we can talk about alla this?

So, still your brother?

Love,
Jacob

*(He folds up the letter, and sits in a spell staring at
it. He tries to keep his emotions at bay; he may or
may not succeed. After several beats, the lights close
in their focus on the actor, illuminating this single
man who now stares directly at the audience. He
continues his fixed stare as all fades to black. Play
time's over.)*

Dan Bernitt's solo performances (*Moments of Disconnect*; *Thanks for the Scabies, Jerkface!*; *Phi Alpha Gamma*) have been featured in theatre festivals across the United States: from Minneapolis and Cape Cod to Cincinnati and New York. He is a recipient of artist development grants and fellowships from the Kentucky Center for the Arts, the University of Kentucky, and the Kentucky Arts Council. His first book, *Dose: Plays & Monologues*, was a finalist for the Lambda Literary Award in Drama.

A Gaines Fellow and member of the Honors Program, he is a summa cum laude graduate of the University of Kentucky's arts administration program. He has also served as creative writing assistant faculty for the Kentucky Governor's School for the Arts, a program of which he is a graduate.

He lives in New York City, where he is a student in the playwriting program at The New School for Drama.

www.danbernitt.com

Printed in the United States
154217LV00001B/130/P